Steck-Vaughn
Comprehension Skills

Conclusion 2

by Donna Townsend
Linda Ward Beech
Tara McCarthy

STECK-VAUGHN COMPANY

AUSTIN, TEXAS
A Division of National Education Corporation

Project Design and Supervision: The Quarasan Group, Inc.
Northfield, Illinois, U.S.A.

Cover and Title Page Photograph: COMSTOCK INC./Tom Grill

ISBN 0–8114–1960–6
Copyright © 1987 by Steck-Vaughn Company, Austin, Texas. All rights reserved. No part of
this book may be reproduced in any form or by any means, electronic or mechanical, including
photocopying, recording, or by any information storage and retrieval system, without written
permission of the publisher. Printed and bound in the United States of America.

4 5 6 7 8 9 0 VP 90 89 88

Drawing a conclusion means using the information you know to make a good guess.

For instance, look at the picture. The man in the picture is working. What is his occupation? Suppose you heard the applause of the audience after the man finished what he was doing. Would that information change your conclusion? Which parts of the picture help you guess the man's job?

What is a conclusion?

A conclusion is a guess you make after thinking about all the information you have. For instance what if you heard that lightning usually strikes tall objects? You could draw the conclusion that climbing a tall tree during a storm is not safe.

The conclusions are not stated in the stories in this book. You draw the conclusions based upon what you know and what you have learned by reading.

Try It!

Read this story about tornados and think about what you can tell from the information in it.

> A tornado is a huge, powerful storm. The rapidly spinning cloud is sometimes called a *funnel cloud* because of its shape. It whirls and spins in the sky and sometimes touches the ground. A tornado has been known to drive a piece of straw through the trunk of a tree.

What conclusion can you draw about a tornado coming toward a city? Write a conclusion on the lines.

_____

_____

You might have written something like: "A tornado coming toward a city can be very dangerous," or "If people in a city see a tornado, they should warn others." You can draw these conclusions from the information in the paragraph. The paragraph says that the tornado is a very powerful storm. The third sentence tells you that these dangerous storms sometimes touch the ground. Based on these facts from the paragraph, you can draw a conclusion.

Practice drawing conclusions

This book asks you to draw a conclusion from the information given in a story. Here is an example:

> Many flowers give off lovely scents. Butterflies fly to flowers to sip the fragrant nectar. You would think that the world's largest flower would make the air for miles around smell good. Instead this three-foot-wide *monster flower* smells just like rotting garbage. Flies buzz around the giant plant all day.

Now, read this question:

a You can guess that:
  a. flies might like monster-flower nectar
  b. butterflies probably like the monster flower
  c. most people like to plant monster flowers in gardens
  d. the monster flower was discovered in 1935

The correct answer is *a*. The paragraph says, "Butterflies fly to flowers to sip the fragrant nectar." Then the paragraph tells how bad the monster flower smells. The last sentence says, "Flies buzz around the giant plant all day long." You can guess that since butterflies sip nectar from the sweet-smelling plants, then flies might drink a bad-smelling nectar from the monster flower.

Sometimes a question asks about something you *cannot* tell from a paragraph. Here is an example:

> Where the Mississippi River flows into the sea, summers are long and hot. There, people working in the fields found a way to make the long, hot days pass more quickly. They sang songs called *hollers*. Near the turn of the century people began singing hollers and playing a guitar. And that is how the music called *the blues* came to be.

Write the letter of the correct answer in the blank.

_____ From this paragraph you cannot tell:
  a. where the blues began
  b. how jazz was born
  c. when the blues began
  d. where summers are hot

3

Conclusions and you

Read the stories on this page. Look at the sentences in each story and try to figure out what the story is about. Finally draw a conclusion about where the person who is telling the story is.

I am wearing a new suit. My hair is combed. I got lost but I drove around until I found the place. I tucked some important papers under my arm, put on my best smile, and opened the office door.

Where am I? _____

First you drop your money in the slot. Then you hold the hose. The water comes out very fast, so don't put your hand in it. You can spray soap on the car, rub the car with a brush, then rinse it off.

Where am I? _____

A car zooms by. Then a noisy bus passes. If only the light would hurry up and change. I must return the books before closing time.

Where am I? _____

All I can hear is the wind. There is no traffic here, and I am up so high that the air is thin. I breathe big breaths of it into my lungs. I think I'll have a snack before I climb any higher. I am almost at the top, but I cannot make it there before lunchtime.

Where am I? _____

How to use this book

This book has 25 units with 5 stories in each unit. After you read each story, choose a reasonable conclusion from the possible answers.

When you finish reading and answering the questions, check your answers by looking at pages 60 through 62. Tear out the answer pages and fold them to the unit you are checking. Write the number of correct answers in the *score* box at the top of the unit page. After you finish all of the stories, try "Conclusion: Just for Fun" on pages 56 through 59.

Hints for Better Reading

■ Read the question carefully. Each question is different. Does the question use the word *not* or the contraction *n't*?

■ Sometimes the clue to the right answer lies in the middle of the story. As you look for the answer, read the whole story again and again.

■ Read all the answers before choosing the right one. Some answers are almost right, but only one of them really fits the facts in the story.

Challenge Yourself

Are you a good reader? Try this special challenge. Read each story and then answer the question about it. Then if the question asks for a conclusion you *can* tell about the paragraph, try to write a conclusion you *cannot* tell from the paragraph. If the question asks for a conclusion you *cannot* tell from the paragraph, write a conclusion you *can* tell from the paragraph.

Unit 1

1. A gorilla named Koko learned sign language. One day, Koko pulled two fingers across her cheeks to indicate whiskers. She wanted a kitten. So she was given one. Now, Koko cuddles and strokes All Ball like a mother gorilla would stroke a tiny baby gorilla. She dresses All Ball in linen napkins and hats. They also tickle each other. How does Koko feel about All Ball? "Soft good cat cat," she says in sign language.

2. Thomas Jefferson's home, Monticello, is famous. But too many people visited the president there. Jefferson could not turn guests away. So he had another home near Lynchburg, Virginia. It was called Poplar Forest, and Jefferson went there when Monticello got too crowded.

3. The abacus is an ancient device made of beads that slide on sticks. It is widely thought that the abacus was only used by storekeepers and money changers in Asia. In fact, the abacus was also used in ancient Rome and Greece. It is still used by waiters in Russia to figure a customer's bill.

4. Two brothers were traveling West in a covered wagon in the 1800's. They grew to detest each other so much that one brother sawed the wagon in half and drove off. He left his brother stranded on the prairie with the back half of the wagon and one set of oxen.

5. Doug Seuss trains bears to wreck cabins and chase pioneers in the movies. But the animal trainer believes the beasts are affectionate and smart. He romps in the creek with his 1,300-pound friend, Bart. Bart rides in the back of Doug's pickup truck to the car wash. That's where the bear takes a bath.

Score ☐

_____ **1.** From this paragraph, you can tell that:
  a. kittens like to wear hats
  b. Koko hates to tickle animals
  c. gorillas can be loving and intelligent
  d. baby gorillas have whiskers

_____ **2.** You can tell that to Jefferson, Poplar Forest was:
  a. a place to get away from the heat at Monticello
  b. a chance to be a real farmer
  c. a place he liked better than Monticello
  d. a place to be alone

_____ **3.** From this story, you can tell that an abacus:
  a. is used to print money
  b. is used to do math
  c. is an invention of the Greeks
  d. is no longer used today

_____ **4.** The brother that was left behind probably thought:
  a. "This trip is not boy's play."
  b. "Remember that time is money."
  c. "This trip surely is fun."
  d. "Money makes the world go around."

_____ **5.** From the story, you can tell that:
  a. bears rarely take baths
  b. Bart doesn't like pickups
  c. Doug is probably a good animal trainer
  d. Bart weighs less than Doug

Unit 2

1. The male bowerbird of Australia courts his mate inside a colorful playhouse. First the bird builds a kind of castle made of towers, huts, and pathways. He decorates this den with butterfly wings, flowers, shells, and stones. Then he waits for the female bowerbird to admire his work.

2. Americans use about three billion barrels of oil a year. Experts are concerned because we use so much. At the rate we are going, we will run out of oil in about seventy years. And it takes nature about two million years to make all the oil we use in one year.

3. Surgeon George Hamilton went down with a ship off the coast of Australia in 1791. Years later when divers examined the wreck, they found the doctor's silver pocket watch stopped at twelve minutes past eleven. They also found a small bottle with an oily liquid in it. It contained oil of cloves used by the doctor. The liquid was still fragrant after almost two hundred years in the ocean.

4. Weather experts can now predict rain, snow, and sunshine fairly well. Some scientists are sure they will soon be able to predict where lightning will strike. Then they can warn airplane pilots to change their routes. Also, people in charge of golf tournaments can adjust their playing schedule.

5. The planet Saturn is famous for the rings around it. The rings are formed of tiny pieces of matter flowing around the planet. The space ship *Voyager 2* has shown that gravity pulls the pieces away from the ring. They fall down towards Saturn. The more pieces fall, the less "ring" there is.

_____ **1.** From this story, you can tell that the male bowerbird:
   a. cannot fly very far
   b. builds its bower to keep out the rain and heat
   c. is a coastal bird that eats fish
   d. builds its bower to attract a mate

_____ **2.** From this story, you can tell that:
   a. Americans use more oil than all the rest of the world
   b. all the oil in this country equals three billion barrels
   c. we will run out of oil in about two million years
   d. we can't expect nature to make enough new oil soon

_____ **3.** From the story you can assume that:
   a. glass helps preserve liquids under water
   b. surgeon Hamilton had many children
   c. the divers found the wreck at 11:12
   d. small bottles hold liquids better than big bottles

_____ **4.** From this story, you can tell that:
   a. experts can now predict where lightning will strike
   b. airplanes aren't affected by lightning
   c. experts are usually in charge of tournaments
   d. lightning is a common danger at golf tournaments

_____ **5.** This story suggests that:
   a. Saturn may not always have its rings
   b. Saturn is the only planet to have rings
   c. Voyager 2 changed the rings of Saturn
   d. gravity is what keeps the rings in place

9

1. There's a mouse club in England. The club members judge the mice on such important qualities as length of their bodies, length of their tails, shape of their ears, and the brightness of their eyes. The show career for mice is ten to twelve months, and the background of each mouse is recorded like a racehorse's.

2. One day two disc jockeys were talking about how fast a driver can go before getting a ticket. The next day, one of the disc jockeys said there was a police officer giving tickets on a particular street. The other DJ wanted to know how the first one knew this. The first one said, "Believe me. They give tickets if you go 62 miles per hour."

3. A gland about the size of a pea controls how tall or short you are. But too much of this gland's growth fluid causes the bones to grow very long and large. The tallest person ever measured grew to be eight feet eleven inches tall and weighed 490 pounds.

4. A baseball batter has less than one tenth of a second to decide what type of pitch is coming. Then the brain has to figure out whether or not to swing. The brain also has to tell the batter's muscles what to do to hit the ball.

5. One scientist thinks studying should be "an active process." He thinks that making fun of the book you're reading helps you remember it later. Don't study in the bedroom, the kitchen, or near a TV. You'll wind up sleeping, eating, or watching. Instead, go to a library or some other place that will help you think.

_____ **1.** These mice probably:
   a. have ears shaped like cauliflowers
   b. live for five years
   c. are judges
   d. have papers showing their backgrounds

_____ **2.** From this story, you might guess:
   a. the disc jockeys like their work
   b. all drivers get speeding tickets
   c. the first disc jockey got a ticket
   d. police officers like to give tickets

_____ **3.** You might guess that too little growth fluid:
   a. makes people very beautiful
   b. causes bones to be shorter than usual
   c. causes people to grow big muscles
   d. makes the hands grow big

_____ **4.** A baseball player:
   a. should be able to think fast
   b. has ten seconds to decide about a pitch
   c. must have muscles that think
   d. always pitches very quickly

_____ **5.** To study actively, you should:
   a. read the material
   b. make a snack and eat it in your bedroom
   c. memorize lists
   d. talk back to the book

1. A duck in a city park in Frieburg, Germany, began to squawk and flap its wings one night during World War II. The duck had once done this just before bombs were dropped. This time, people heard the duck and ran for cover. The bombing soon began. Today in the park, there is a statue of the duck. It died in the attack.

2. Mack Sennett was an early film director who was famous for his silent comedies. Sennett's films about the Keystone Cops ignored the logic of everyday life. The Keystone Cops rarely arrested anyone. If they did, it was the wrong person. The lovely girls in Sennett's movies fell in love with ugly men instead of cute ones. His films often ended in horrible scenes where no one got hurt.

3. Did you ever wake up just before your alarm clock rang? Experts know that people have inner clocks in their bodies. The clock divides time into about 24 hours. Jet lag, or feeling tired and grumpy, is a result of upsetting that inner clock.

4. Most movies show burglars studying a place before they strike. The movies show burglars picking locks with great skill. But police departments say that most burglars are very crude. They look for unlocked doors. If they don't find any, they just break the door, the lock, or the window. Then they work fast.

5. The Baseball Hall of Fame is in Cooperstown, N.Y. It is there because that is where Abner Doubleday said he invented the game in 1839. Actually, baseball began in England from a game called "rounders." The word "baseball" is mentioned in English books as early as 1798.

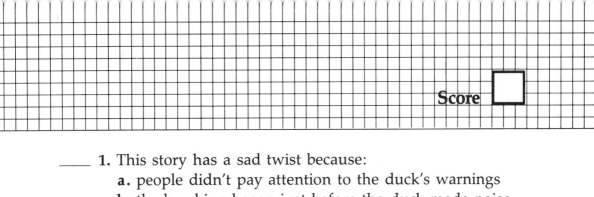

_____ **1.** This story has a sad twist because:
   a. people didn't pay attention to the duck's warnings
   b. the bombing began just before the duck made noise
   c. the duck was killed in the attack after warning people about it
   d. the statue doesn't look anything like the duck

_____ **2.** Actors in Mack Sennett's films did not
   a. have to speak
   b. like working
   c. laugh a lot at work
   d. often fall in love

_____ **3.** From this story, you can tell that jet lag:
   a. happens when a person's inner clock is off schedule
   b. has nothing to do with the body's inner clock
   c. goes away after you reset your watch
   d. is something experts rarely suffer from

_____ **4.** From this story, you can tell that:
   a. the police have no way to stop burglars
   b. burglars are usually skilled at what they do
   c. burglars plan robberies carefully
   d. burglars in movies are not true-to-life

_____ **5.** This story suggests that Abner Doubleday:
   a. began a game called "rounders"
   b. invented the word "baseball" but not the game
   c. invented the game but not the word "baseball"
   d. took credit for something he didn't really do

1. Jim clutched the wheel so tightly his knuckles stuck out against his skin. The woman next to him turned the key, and said, "Now just start out slowly down the street. You only need to turn the wheel slightly to change direction." Jim pressed his foot down carefully.

2. Roberta put the key in the slot and turned it. Inside the little box were four envelopes, which she pulled out. She flipped through the first three quickly, muttering, "bill," at each of the three. At the fourth envelope she stopped, grinned, and ripped open the flap.

3. The first drop sent up a tiny cloud of dust and then disappeared. A rattlesnake slithered away from the unexpected sight. More drops followed, but they too were quickly lost in the dry sand. Then the drops increased and puddles began to form between the cactus plants.

4. It was six by the time they reached Topeka, Kansas. Jed announced that they were now halfway there. "Another couple of days," he said, "and we will be swimming in the Pacific Ocean." He said it to cheer up the kids, but they were so tired of being in the car that nothing could cheer them up.

5. As they came outside, Marianne told Cathy that the ending had surprised her. Cathy said the ending hadn't surprised her, but she didn't understand why the police took so long to question the maid. Marianne asked Cathy if she was hungry, but Cathy said she had eaten too much popcorn.

_____ **1.** You can tell from this story that Jim:
    a. is teaching the woman to drive
    b. is relaxed and confident
    c. is learning how to drive from the woman
    d. is leaving the dock in a motorboat

_____ **2.** From this, you know that Roberta probably:
    a. gets a lot of letters from a friend named Bill
    b. got three bills
    c. got money in the fourth envelope
    d. gets a lot of mail every day

_____ **3.** This is a description of:
    a. rain falling in a desert after a dry period
    b. the sprinkler system going on in a zoo
    c. someone watering a lawn
    d. a storm beginning in the mountains

_____ **4.** You can tell that the family:
    a. is moving to a new town
    b. has already been on the road a few days
    c. is moving from Topeka, Kansas
    d. has never seen the Pacific Ocean

_____ **5.** From this story, you can guess that Marianne and Cathy:
    a. have just finished a meal at a restaurant
    b. just met
    c. are police officers discussing a case
    d. have just seen a movie together

15

1. In Tarzan movies, quicksand pulls victims down to their certain deaths. Quicksand actually does not suck people into it at all. In fact, it is impossible for a person to sink all the way down in quicksand. However, people may drown after losing their balance.

2. There is a strange boat race every year in Australia's Todd River. A pair of racers stands inside a boat without a bottom. Then they run down the riverbed holding the boat by its sides. The race was cancelled one year when an unusual amount of rain actually filled the Todd River with water.

3. Pete Gray wanted to play baseball even though he had lost his right arm at the age of six. He began playing professional baseball in 1943. Two years later he was playing center field with the St. Louis Browns. He batted well, stole bases regularly, and was a good fielder.

4. There is actually a summer camp for dogs in Margaretsville, New York. The counselors have treasure hunts for dogs by hiding dog biscuits. The camp sends regular reports on the dogs to their owners. Each report is signed with the dog's pawprint.

5. One difference between an alligator and a crocodile is that the alligator has a much larger snout. Also, the alligator has an overbite. This means the teeth in its lower jaw fit behind the teeth of its upper jaw. But the bottom and top teeth of the crocodile fit between each other, forming a single row when closed.

_____ 1. You can tell from this story that:
  a. people can swim in quicksand
  b. quicksand is accurately shown in movies
  c. movies exaggerate the danger of quicksand
  d. if you fall in quicksand you can never get out

_____ 2. From this story, you know that:
  a. the water of the river will hold up a bottomless boat
  b. Australia always has plenty of rain
  c. the Todd River is usually dry
  d. the race will become part of the summer Olympics

_____ 3. From this you can tell that Gray:
  a. was determined to play baseball
  b. played professional baseball more than three years
  c. lost his arm in an accident
  d. played professional baseball longer than most players

_____ 4. From this, you can probably guess that the dogs:
  a. learn weaving and crafts on rainy days
  b. often get homesick
  c. are owned by people who spoil their dogs
  d. are taught tricks by the counselors

_____ 5. To tell a crocodile and an alligator apart, you would:
  a. look at their tails
  b. have to feel their tails
  c. have to see their eyes
  d. have to see their mouths

Unit 7

1. Only one president was arrested for speeding while in office. A police officer stopped Ulysses S. Grant when he was driving a horse and buggy too fast. This was not even Grant's first offense. He was fined five dollars twice before for breaking the speed limit.

2. Tomatoes used to be thought of as poisonous, perhaps because of their bright color. In 1820, a man in Salem, New Jersey proved they weren't harmful. Robert Johnson ate an entire basket of tomatoes in front of the whole town. His doctor was there and was sure that Johnson would die.

3. Many people believe that margarine was invented during World War II. This substitute for butter was actually made by the French in 1869. It wasn't used widely in the U.S. because dairy farmers were against its sale. The last law against it, in Wisconsin, ended in 1967.

4. The *W* was called a *hook* thousands of years ago. Back then it was shaped like the letter *Y*. The Romans drew the *W* like the letter *V*. Some people in the Middle Ages drew the *W* as two *V*'s side-by-side. Other people at this time drew the letter as *UU*.

5. Mechanical clocks are about seven hundred years old. But daily time was measured as long as three thousand years ago. The Egyptians measured time with a shadow stick. It cast a shadow across markers as the sun moved. Another "clock" was a candle marked with numbers.

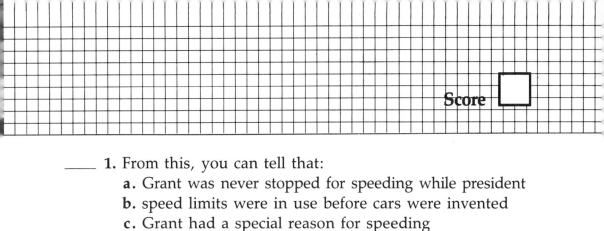

_____ **1.** From this, you can tell that:
   a. Grant was never stopped for speeding while president
   b. speed limits were in use before cars were invented
   c. Grant had a special reason for speeding
   d. the speed limit was five miles per hour then

_____ **2.** From this, you can tell that:
   a. brightly colored plants may be poisonous
   b. tomatoes are usually dull-looking
   c. Robert Johnson was afraid he would die
   d. Robert Johnson's doctor liked tomatoes

_____ **3.** You can tell from this story that:
   a. dairy farmers approved of the use of margarine
   b. Wisconsin probably has a lot of dairy farmers
   c. French dairy farmers opposed the use of margarine
   d. margarine was widely used in the U.S. before 1967

_____ **4.** The letter _W_ got its name because it once:
   a. looked like the letter _V_
   b. was used by the Romans
   c. was written _UU_
   d. was called a _hook_

_____ **5.** You can tell from the story that:
   a. you can use a shadow stick at night
   b. the Egyptians were interested in mechanical clocks
   c. people have always been interested in measuring time
   d. people have always measured time with candles

Unit 8

1. Don't let anyone ever tell you that they went out with a fishing pole and caught a sardine. The name sardine doesn't apply to any one kind of fish by itself. It is used to describe any small fish that can be canned. Young herring are often used as sardines.

2. The words of our national song, "The Star-Spangled Banner," were written by Francis Scott Key. He wrote the words during the war America fought against the British in 1812. It is interesting to know that the tune is not original. It was taken from a British music-hall song popular at the time.

3. A New Yorker invented something called a *Scootboard*. It is like the scooters children stand on and push with one foot. But the Scootboard has a bicycle wheel in front with an engine attached. The person standing on the narrow platform uses hand controls and can go 30 miles per hour.

4. The stories of wolves attacking and eating human beings are false. There is not one recorded case of a wolf attacking a human in North America. Only a wolf with rabies would bite a human being. And rabies is a disease that strikes dogs and foxes as well.

5. Some words in our language have changed meanings over the centuries. For example, the word *liquor* once meant any kind of liquid, even water. The word *meat* once meant any kind of food at all. And in England in the fourteenth century, *girl* meant either a young man or woman.

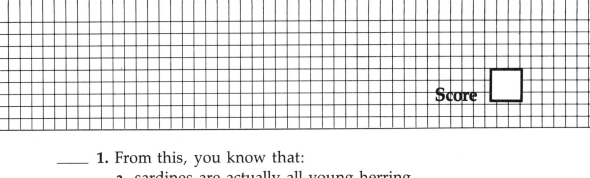

_____ **1.** From this, you know that:
    a. sardines are actually all young herring
    b. sardines like to go fishing
    c. the word _sardine_ doesn't refer to a canned fish
    d. a person might find young herring in a sardine can

_____ **2.** Our national song is interesting because:
    a. Francis Scott Key didn't write it
    b. it was written during a war
    c. it was taken from America's enemy at the time
    d. it is difficult for most people to sing

_____ **3.** You probably you haven't seen many Scootboards because:
    a. hand controls direct the engine
    b. they may not be safe
    c. they can go 30 miles per hour
    d. most Scootboard owners are children

_____ **4.** From this story, you can tell that:
    a. wolves are dangerous to human beings
    b. there is only one case of a wolf attacking a human
    c. there are few wolves in North America
    d. wolves are no more dangerous than dogs

_____ **5.** The older meanings of these words were:
    a. more narrow than today's meanings
    b. broader than today's meanings
    c. not related to today's meanings
    d. changed after the fourteenth century

1. The potato has traveled a lot. It was first grown by the Inca people of South America. Spanish explorers took the plant from there to Europe, where it grew well. Then the Europeans settled North America. When they did, they brought potatoes back to this side of the Atlantic Ocean.

2. An artist named Kurt Ossenfort produces unusual drawings. They are made by trees. He sets up the easel and canvas next to a tree he likes. Then he ties a pen to the tip of a branch so that it touches the canvas. The wind blows the pen around. His favorite drawing is by a white oak.

3. In Africa it is common to see women carrying heavy loads on their heads. Scientists are surprised at how little energy these woman use. A male army recruit carrying 70 percent of his body weight on his back uses 100 percent more oxygen to do so. A woman carrying 70 percent of her body weight on her head increases her oxygen use by only 50 percent.

4. The London Bridge from the nursery song was a stone bridge made in the twelfth century. It had shops and homes built onto it. These were always catching on fire or needing repair. The bridge was replaced in the 1800's.

5. Almost all cats purr, but they never purr when they're alone. They purr only around other cats or human beings. That makes animal experts think purring is a form of cat talking. It may be a sign that a cat is willing to submit itself to another cat or person.

_____ 1. You can tell that probably:
   a. the Spaniards brought the first potato to America
   b. the potato is grown only in the mountains
   c. the potato did not take a direct route to North America
   d. there is no way to grow potatoes on both sides of the Atlantic

_____ 2. From this you can tell that:
   a. Kurt Ossenfort is sad
   b. the drawings don't show things the way photographs do
   c. the drawings are all of nearby trees
   d. the drawings are just one dot on each canvas

_____ 3. From this story you can tell that:
   a. army recruits are weaker than African women
   b. scientists are often surprised
   c. it is impossible for women to carry heavy loads
   d. the head carries loads with less energy than the back

_____ 4. From the story, you can tell:
   a. if the people in London liked the bridge
   b. why the homes and shops caught fire
   c. why the song says, "London Bridge is falling down"
   d. why the bridge in the song had shops and homes

_____ 5. This story suggests that:
   a. cats purr when they are relaxed
   b. cats purr when they are fearful
   c. cats always purr when they're alone
   d. purring is a form of breathing

1. Grace opened her eyes. What time was it, she wondered. The room was dark until she drew back the curtains. A mockingbird began its song, and from another room, she smelled burning toast. Her roommate would never learn to set the toaster right, she thought.

2. Jimmy asked Jeanine to help him glue on his false moustache and she asked him if her grey wig looked crooked. They looked across the floor at the old-fashioned furniture lit by the spotlights. When they saw the huge curtain begin to rise and heard the applause, they wished each other luck.

3. The man wriggled his toes in the sand and then returned to the towel on the ground. He picked up the pair of binoculars by the towel and looked through them. The ship in the distance didn't have an American flag. But he couldn't tell what country the flag was from.

4. The two men sat across from each other. Both of them studied the square table between them. The first man picked up a tiny plastic disk and moved it. The second man picked up a different colored disk and slid his in the opposite direction. "Well, I guess you've got me this time," the first man said.

5. The woman led the animal over to me. It snorted and pricked its ears. "Put your left foot here," she said to me, pointing to a metal ring. "Then just swing your leg over Diablo's back and you're on." She handed me the leather straps. "Why," I thought, "does Diablo seem to be smiling?"

_____ 1. From this story, you can tell that Grace:
   a. has awakened from a midday nap
   b. has fallen asleep at school
   c. is waking up in the morning
   d. is going to bed at night

_____ 2. From this, you can tell that:
   a. Jimmy and Jeanine are opening an antique store
   b. Jimmy and Jeanine are watching a movie
   c. Jimmy and Jeanine are about to act in a play
   d. Jimmy and Jeanine are brother and sister

_____ 3. You can tell that the man:
   a. is a spy for a foreign country
   b. is standing on a beach looking out in the ocean
   c. doesn't have very much money
   d. is camping in the mountains during the winter

_____ 4. The two men in this story are probably:
   a. strangers who have recently met
   b. building a radio from a kit
   c. playing a board game like checkers
   d. eating dinner together

_____ 5. From this story, you know that the person telling it
   a. is a good friend of the woman
   b. is about to feed an elephant
   c. is trying to teach a dog a circus trick
   d. is learning how to ride a horse

Unit 11

1.   *Acrophobia* means *fear of heights*. People who feel this fear aren't any less afraid when fences or railings protect them. Their fear is not just one of falling. People who suffer from acrophobia may be afraid that they will want to jump from the height.

2.   Most slaves don't become famous. But Aesop was unusual. He was a clever and witty Greek slave who earned his freedom with his cleverness. He used his animal fables to teach people to respect the rights of others. Two thousand years later, people still use his stories to teach lessons or gain helpful advice.

3.   The akita is a Japanese hunting dog with short, bristly hair. It is considered a symbol of good health. In fact, the dog is so prized it has been made an official national treasure. The first akita to enter the U.S. was brought by Helen Keller, the blind and deaf author, in 1937.

4.   The anableps is a freshwater fish found in Mexico and parts of South America. It is unusual because of its eyes. A band of skin divides each of its eyes into halves, giving it four eyes. It stays near the top of the water, looking above and below the water at the same time.

5.   The keyboard of today's typewriter was first set up to slow down the speed of typing. The first typists would type too fast. Then the typewriters would jam. So the designer put the keys the way they are today to force the typists to go slower.

_____ 1. From this story, you can tell that:
   a. people with this fear probably don't like to work in tall buildings
   b. many people suffer from acrophobia
   c. fences make people with this fear feel better
   d. people can get over acrophobia

_____ 2. From this, you can tell that:
   a. some Greeks were slaves
   b. the Greek people never freed a slave
   c. people have finally learned to respect others
   d. many slaves become famous after they're free

_____ 3. From this, you know that akitas:
   a. are bred in Northern Japan
   b. were brought to the U.S. before 1937
   c. are valued for more than their hunting ability
   d. became very popular in the United States

_____ 4. You can assume that the anableps:
   a. needs bifocals
   b. has extremely sensitive skin
   c. can't be caught with a rod and reel
   d. hunts for food above and below the water

_____ 5. From this, you can tell that:
   a. the arrangement of keys affects the speed of typing
   b. the designer did not know much about typing
   c. typewriters today use a different arrangement of keys
   d. the arrangement of keys doesn't affect typing speed

1. The giant saguaro cactus plant is often seen in Western movies. Although the largest plants can grow to be 50 feet tall, they grow very slowly at first. The stem of the plant grows about one inch its first ten years, but later it grows at a faster rate. The largest can live for almost two hundred years.

2. You have seen the movies where the Roman Emperor shows that a gladiator should die by turning down his thumb. Actually, the gory Roman custom was to turn a thumb up toward the heart for death. Thumbs down meant that the soldier should be allowed to live.

3. In New York's Federal Reserve Bank, workers handle money and other valuable metals. One of the heaviest things workers must carry is a gold brick. For this reason, some of them wear special shoes made of magnesium. These shoes protect workers' toes if a brick falls on them.

4. Sleepwalking is most common among children ten to twelve years old. Experts think it is linked to the growth and development of children. People who sleepwalk can easily hurt themselves. They also may be so confused that they try to strike people who wake them.

5. Elizabeth Tashjian runs the world's only nut museum. The museum is on the first floor of an old mansion, which is also her home. Her collection of nuts from around the world is always being raided by bushy-tailed thieves who live near the house.

_____ **1.** From this information, you can figure out:
  a. why the cactus grows slowly at first
  b. why the cactus is in the movies
  c. exactly what the cactus looks like
  d. how fast the stem grows the first ten years

_____ **2.** From this, you can tell that death probably occurred:
  a. once out of every five times
  b. when the Emperor put his thumb down
  c. when the Emperor put his thumb up
  d. only in the movies, and not in real-life Rome

_____ **3.** From this story, you can tell that magnesium:
  a. is a harder metal than gold
  b. is a softer metal than gold
  c. is a more valuable metal than gold
  d. is a more comfortable material than leather

_____ **4.** From this story, you know that you should:
  a. always try to wake someone who is sleepwalking
  b. be careful when waking a sleepwalker
  c. expect children under eight to sleepwalk
  d. not worry about someone who is sleepwalking

_____ **5.** Elizabeth Tashjian doesn't call the police because:
  a. she doesn't like police officers
  b. the thieves are squirrels and chipmunks
  c. the police don't take her seriously
  d. she feeds the nuts to her horse

29

Unit 13

1. You may think of the contact lens as a fairly new invention. But the first contact lenses were made by a German glassblower in 1887. These contact lenses were ordered by an eye doctor to treat an eye disease. They were made to cover the entire eye.

2. Mussels use a powerful glue to attach themselves to rocks underwater. Now scientists have found a way to make the glue in a laboratory. The glue isn't affected by water or salt. It can be used to glue fillings into teeth. The glue can even be used to join badly broken bones.

3. The Apollo space craft returned to Earth with 843 pounds of moon rocks. Most of them are now in Houston, Texas. People have been looking closely at the rocks. So far, the rocks have not shown where the moon came from. But scientists still borrow pieces to study.

4. The two World Wars were not the wars that took the most American lives. The most costly war in human lives was the Civil War. At least 524,000 soldiers died in that conflict. That number is one fifth more than died in World War II.

5. People sleepwalk only during very deep sleep. If you wake a sleepwalker, he or she will not remember any dreams. People dream during a lighter sleep. The dreamer's closed eyes may move rapidly back and forth. If you see a sleeping person's eyes move and awaken the person, the person may be able to remember vivid dreams.

_____ **1.** From this story, you cannot tell:
     a. what the first contact lenses were for
     b. where the person who made the first pair was from
     c. whether the first contact lenses were successful
     d. how long contact lenses have been in existence

_____ **2.** From this story, you can tell that:
     a. mussels do not have bones or teeth
     b. the glue produced in the laboratory is very expensive
     c. water and salt reduce the strength of most glues
     d. mussels move from one place to another

_____ **3.** You can tell that when the Apollo ship returned, scientists:
     a. knew the origin of the moon
     b. hoped to learn more from moon samples
     c. took the rocks to Washington D.C.
     d. refused to let other people see the rocks

_____ **4.** From this story, you might assume that:
     a. the Civil War lasted one year
     b. World War II ranks just after the Civil War in lives lost
     c. Americans fought in only the three wars mentioned
     d. the American Revolution cost a lot of lives

_____ **5.** You can tell that:
     a. sleepwalkers probably don't dream
     b. the best sleep is very deep
     c. vivid dreams help people sleep
     d. people dream during a deep sleep

Unit 14

1. The Mohawks are native to New York, and they have always shown an original quality. They have no fear of heights and are very nimble. For this reason, most of the skyscrapers in New York City were built by the Mohawk workers. They came in by subway from their settlement in Brooklyn.

2. You may have enough to worry about without worrying about meteorites hitting you. But it does happen. The last victim, in 1954, was Mrs. E. H. Hodges. A nine-pound space rock went through the roof of her house, bounced off a radio, and struck her. She was bruised but not seriously hurt.

3. The song "Old Folks at Home" starts with the line, "Way down upon the Swanee River." Stephen Foster, the song's author, never saw the river. It is actually called the Suwannee and is in Florida. The name Suwannee was a way of saying the river's original name, the *San Juan*.

4. On Uranus, the seventh planet, the seas may be made of boiling water. The air glows in the dark. The days are just about seventeen hours long, and the temperature of the air may be about four hundred degrees below freezing.

5. The Museum of Modern Art in New York may be thought of as the authority on modern art. In 1961 it got some new works by the French artist Henri Matisse. One of these paintings was "Le Bateau" ("The Boat"). The painting hung in the museum for 47 days before someone noticed it was upside down.

32

____ **1.** You cannot tell from this story:
   a. where the Mohawks who worked on skyscrapers lived
   b. what special quality the Mohawks possess
   c. why the Mohawks were hired to work on skyscrapers
   d. how many Mohawks worked on the skyscrapers

____ **2.** You know the danger of meteorites is slight because:
   a. they are so small
   b. Mrs. Hodges was reading a book
   c. they fall so rarely
   d. people spend most of their time indoors

____ **3.** To be true to history, Stephen Foster should have:
   a. sailed on the river before writing the song
   b. written, "Down by the old folks at home"
   c. written, "Way down upon the San Juan River"
   d. written, "Way down upon the Swanee River"

____ **4.** From the paragraph, you can guess that you should:
   a. take a coat to visit Uranus
   b. know why the air glows
   c. know how many seas there are
   d. know that Uranus is a pleasant place to visit

____ **5.** From this story, you can tell that:
   a. the painting was not really by Henri Matisse
   b. the painting probably didn't look like a boat
   c. the museum people didn't like French art
   d. the painting didn't belong in the museum

33

1. Even though she had read the signs, Sally reached out her hand. She stretched forward with the popcorn held out in the tips of her fingers. The soft mouth of the striped animal just fit through the bars to reach the popcorn. It nibbled greedily.

2. The shaggy little animal went up to the back door. It rattled the screen door with its front paw, and then sat down. It was quiet for awhile. But soon a face appeared at the door, and then there was a scream of joy. "It's Goldie!" a girl's voice said. "She's come back."

3. Becky came downstairs in the morning. "I don't like this house at all," the girl told her parents. "It smells funny." Her mother asked her if she had seen the wild strawberries growing in the front. Her father mentioned a pony he had seen at the neighboring house. The girl's eyes lit up.

4. The man tried to balance but he wobbled. The wheels seemed to go in every direction at once. When he hit a bump, his foot lost its grip on the pedal. He sat straight up on the narrow seat with his arms forward. "I haven't done this in a long time," he said with a laugh.

5. Bernice dabbed at the nose first with short little strokes. Then she brushed near the ears. She wanted to finish the face before the sun set. She realized she needed a deeper shadow under the man's eyes, and dipped her brush again. She touched the brush to the canvas.

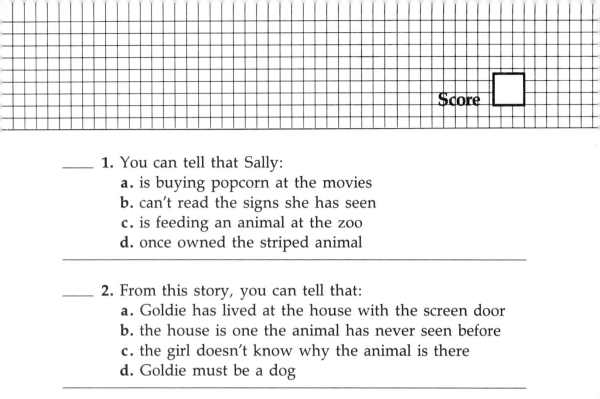

_____ 1. You can tell that Sally:
   a. is buying popcorn at the movies
   b. can't read the signs she has seen
   c. is feeding an animal at the zoo
   d. once owned the striped animal

_____ 2. From this story, you can tell that:
   a. Goldie has lived at the house with the screen door
   b. the house is one the animal has never seen before
   c. the girl doesn't know why the animal is there
   d. Goldie must be a dog

_____ 3. You can probably assume that this family:
   a. is about to move to a new house
   b. has just moved to this house
   c. will leave the house because of Becky's feelings
   d. will punish Becky for being rude

_____ 4. The man is:
   a. driving a car for the first time in a long time
   b. trying to use a mixer in the kitchen
   c. trying to ride a unicycle
   d. trying to ride a bicycle

_____ 5. You can tell that Bernice:
   a. works as a makeup artist
   b. is helping a patient at a hospital wash his face
   c. is painting a picture of a man
   d. is cleaning an ancient mask

35

1. At one time, there were less than one hundred trumpeter swans left in the world. The giant birds were hunted for their skin and quills. Their soft feathers were used in powder puffs. But people began to watch out for the graceful swans. Now about ten thousand of these majestic birds are left.

2. July 4 is a very American day. The Declaration of Independence was signed on that day. President Calvin Coolidge was born on it. Three Presidents died on it. John Adams and Thomas Jefferson died in 1826. James Monroe died in 1831. Also, work on the Washington Monument was begun on July 4, 1848.

3. The shrew is the smallest mammal in the world. It has to eat its own weight in food every day to stay alive. One of the laws of nature is that the smaller a mammal is, the more it must eat in proportion to its size.

4. D-Day occurred in June 1944 when Allied troops invaded France. The Germans wanted to find out where the invasion would take place. Their spy planes saw hundreds of tanks and jeeps and an oil refinery at one place in England. They reported this build-up. But the vehicles were inflated rubber, and the oil refinery was a fake, put together by movie-set designers. The fakes were not part of the real invasion.

5. The name of a city on an island in the Pacific Ocean is written *Pago Pago*, but is pronounced *Pango Pango*. The missionaries who came to the island printed the name of the town in Latin. But they didn't have enough *n*'s in their sets of type, so they left the *n*'s out of the town's name.

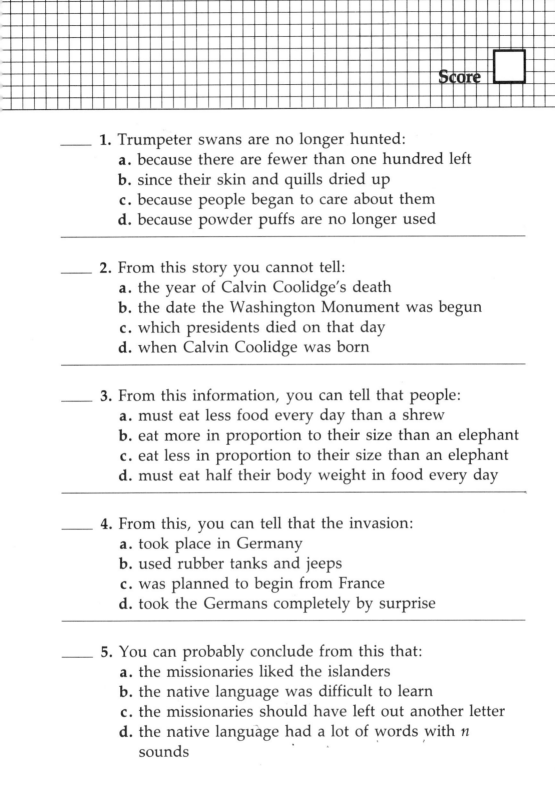

_____ 1. Trumpeter swans are no longer hunted:
    a. because there are fewer than one hundred left
    b. since their skin and quills dried up
    c. because people began to care about them
    d. because powder puffs are no longer used

_____ 2. From this story you cannot tell:
    a. the year of Calvin Coolidge's death
    b. the date the Washington Monument was begun
    c. which presidents died on that day
    d. when Calvin Coolidge was born

_____ 3. From this information, you can tell that people:
    a. must eat less food every day than a shrew
    b. eat more in proportion to their size than an elephant
    c. eat less in proportion to their size than an elephant
    d. must eat half their body weight in food every day

_____ 4. From this, you can tell that the invasion:
    a. took place in Germany
    b. used rubber tanks and jeeps
    c. was planned to begin from France
    d. took the Germans completely by surprise

_____ 5. You can probably conclude from this that:
    a. the missionaries liked the islanders
    b. the native language was difficult to learn
    c. the missionaries should have left out another letter
    d. the native language had a lot of words with n sounds

37

1. The name *John Wayne* is often used to describe a perfect soldier or military hero. The actor John Wayne did make movies in which he played tough, strong soldiers. But oddly enough, he never actually served in the armed forces.

2. Are the names Paul, John, Ringo, and George familiar to you? They were members of the famous rock group called the *Beatles*. At first the Beatles were influenced by the songs of Elvis Presley and Chuck Berry. Later they gave us a type of rock music all their own.

3. Experts study people who are good at influencing others. They find that people with influence can figure out what other people want and why they want it. They can do this even when the people say they want something else or give reasons that aren't the real ones.

4. We all use the phrase, "national holiday" for days like July 4 and Labor Day. But there are no such holidays. The Federal government does not have the power to make one day a holiday for the whole country. Each state votes on whether to make a certain day a legal holiday.

5. Scientists used to think that the praying mantis was deaf. Now they know that a praying mantis has one ear near its stomach. No other creature of any kind is known to have only one ear.

_____ 1. From this story, it is impossible to tell:
    a. what kinds of roles John Wayne played in the movies
    b. what kind of person the name *John Wayne* describes
    c. whether John Wayne served in the armed forces
    d. why John Wayne never served in the armed forces

_____ 2. You can suppose that the Beatles:
    a. were born in South America
    b. became famous after Elvis Presley
    c. liked each other a lot
    d. wrote "Love Me Tender"

_____ 3. This quality of people with influence might be called:
    a. "not seeing the forest for the trees"
    b. "finding a diamond in the rough"
    c. "seeing beneath the surface"
    d. "making the best of a bad thing"

_____ 4. From this story, you know that:
    a. there are no holidays celebrated by all states
    b. there is no holiday celebrated by one state alone
    c. a national holiday should be called a state holiday
    d. all states celebrate the same holidays

_____ 5. From this, you can tell that the way the insect hears:
    a. is not its most unusual feature
    b. was not easy for scientists to understand
    c. is with its stomach
    d. is the same way people hear

39

Unit *18*

1. No one is sure where the word *blimp* comes from. During World War I, the giant balloons were used to catch enemy submarines. As the blimp floated across the sky, the blimp's pilot would see if the blimp had enough gas to keep it up in the air. The pilot would thump the side of the balloon with a thumb. The sound the pilot heard was *blimp*.

2. Handwriting can be turned into a form of art called *calligraphy*. *Calligraphy* means *beautiful writing*. Each stroke of the artist's pen or brush makes beautiful ornaments out of letters. Examples of calligraphy are shown in many art museums.

3. There is a bird in India called the tailorbird. It is called this because it sews a nest for its eggs. The bird finds two leaves close together at the end of a branch. It punches holes with its beak along the edges of the leaves. Then it uses natural fibers to sew the leaves into a pocket.

4. One architect thinks that buildings in America are turning into forts. Many city buildings have blank, windowless walls along the street. These buildings are made for protection against crime. But the architect thinks they make cities less human. This may lead to more crime.

5. A leap year is one in which February has an extra, or twenty-ninth day. This day is needed because each real year lasts a little longer than 365 days. If the extra day weren't added every few years, someday we would celebrate Christmas in July.

_____ **1.** This story suggests that during World War I:
  a. there were no submarines in use
  b. there was no exact way to measure gas in a blimp
  c. blimps had little military use
  d. blimps were the only aircraft in use

_____ **2.** Museums show calligraphy because it can be:
  a. a good way of making signs for visitors
  b. a work of art
  c. helpful in teaching people how to write
  d. made with brushes and pens

_____ **3.** From this story, you can tell that the tailorbird:
  a. can be found anywhere in the world
  b. was given its name because of the way it flies
  c. must be very large
  d. has a sharp beak

_____ **4.** From the story, you cannot tell:
  a. what the architect likes about city buildings
  b. what many city buildings look like
  c. the effect of blank city buildings on people
  d. why these buildings are made this way

_____ **5.** From this, you know that:
  a. most years on a calendar have a total of 365 days
  b. February has an extra day every twenty-ninth year
  c. it isn't possible to figure out the length of a year
  d. someday Christmas will come in July

Unit 19

1. William James Sidis' father was a Harvard professor who decided to make his son a genius. At two, Sidis could type in English and French. He entered Harvard at age 11, the youngest person ever to do so. After Harvard, he retired from public life, took small jobs, and rarely made over twenty-five dollars a week.

2. Quicksand has its dangers, but it isn't as dangerous as an alkali, or salt, bog. Alkali bogs are dangerous because they are found on hillsides as well as along river beds. Once in an alkali bog, people or animals sink faster than they do in quicksand.

3. George Harbo and Frank Samuelson rowed out of New York Harbor on June 6, 1896 in an eighteen-foot boat. They kept rowing until August 1, when they arrived in England. Their only rest came on July 15, when a freighter took them aboard briefly and gave them fresh food.

4. Charles Goodyear discovered the process that made rubber into a useful product. His early businesses failed, and he began his rubber experiments while in prison for debt. He later sold his ideas about rubber because he had no money. He was poor when he died at the age of 60. He left his family in debt.

5. Scientists know that the world's seas are rising. In the last century, the oceans have risen about four inches. But the United States is also slowly sinking. In the last one hundred years, the sea level of the U.S. has risen about one foot.

_____ **1.** From this information, you cannot tell:
   a. which languages Sidis knew
   b. what Sidis' father did for a living
   c. how Sidis spent his years after graduation
   d. why Sidis was not very successful

_____ **2.** From this, you can assume that quicksand:
   a. is more dangerous than an alkali bog in some ways
   b. usually doesn't occur on hillsides
   c. is nothing to worry about
   d. is not similar to an alkali bog

_____ **3.** The two men probably:
   a. met the freighter in the first half of their trip
   b. rowed without stopping to sleep
   c. never got out of their boat until reaching England
   d. were glad to see the freighter

_____ **4.** From this, you know that Charles Goodyear:
   a. never worked very hard
   b. became a rich man after inventing the rubber process
   c. was cheated out of his fortune
   d. never made money from his important invention

_____ **5.** From this story, you cannot tell:
   a. who knows that the oceans are rising
   b. how long it took the oceans to rise four inches
   c. how much the U.S. has sunk
   d. the cause of the rise in sea level around the world

1. The people inside the huge building heard the long blast of the whistle. Quickly, they stopped their machines. They got up from their chairs and went to their lockers. With paper bags in their hands, they walked into the sunny park to eat.

2. The owner let Robert in. As he did every morning, Robert removed the trash from the night before. Then he made sure things were stacked neatly on the shelves. He counted out money into the cash register. At nine sharp, the owner told him to open the door.

3. The woman waited while the child stood at the glass counter. The boy slid his nose from one end of the counter to the other. His mother tapped her foot more and more impatiently. Behind the counter, a man waited with a scoop in his hand. Finally, the boy spoke. "Vanilla," he said.

4. He heard the steady drumming sound he made on the pavement. One foot was becoming sore, but he didn't acknowledge the pain. At last he passed the park bench with the broken seat. "One more mile to go," he thought.

5. William went inside the small wire fence and knelt down. He gently took a leaf in his fingers. He closely examined the little pattern of holes along one edge. "The rabbits have raided us again," he said to his wife. Then he snapped off the one head of lettuce left, and stood up.

_____ 1. You can tell from this story that the people:
      a. are working and going on their lunch hour
      b. are putting together television sets
      c. have been taking English classes at school
      d. are athletes about to play a big game

_____ 2. From this it is clear that Robert:
      a. enjoys what he is doing
      b. works at a store that opens at 9 A.M.
      c. is helping out at the public library
      d. works at a store that closes at 9 P.M.

_____ 3. You can tell that this story takes place in:
      a. a gas station
      b. a clothing store
      c. an ice cream store
      d. a doctor's office

_____ 4. From this, you can tell that the man:
      a. is running in a gym
      b. is running along a route he often takes
      c. is a stranger to the neighborhood
      d. has broken his foot

_____ 5. From this story, you can tell that the man and his wife:
      a. run a farm for their living
      b. are raising rabbits for pets
      c. are buying food at a grocery store
      d. have a small vegetable garden

1. The poet Longfellow wrote a poem that made Paul Revere famous for his ride to Concord to warn that the British were coming. But actually Revere never made it to Concord. Nor was he alone. Two other riders, William Dawes and Dr. Samuel Prescott, went with him, and it was Prescott who warned Concord.

2. The U.S. is full of small, special museums. There is a Sport Fishing Museum in New York, a museum for locks in Connecticut, and the Maple Museum in Vermont. There is a Lumberman's Museum in Maine, and the Petrified Creatures Museum is in New York.

3. The parasol ant of South America gets its name from the way it carries a bit of leaf over its head. But Native Brazilians call them doctor ants. They use the ants' strong jaws to clamp deep cuts closed. Once the ants' jaws have clamped, the Brazilians pinch off their bodies to keep the wound sealed.

4. In 1883, a mailman in California named Jim Stacy found a stray dog which he called Dorsey. Dorsey went on the mail route with Stacy. But Stacy got sick. So he tied the mail and a note to Dorsey's back and the dog went out alone. Dorsey delivered the mail in this fashion until 1886.

5. The odd-looking dodo bird became extinct shortly after it was found. It was discovered on an island in 1598 by a Dutch admiral. He brought some birds to Europe, where their pictures were painted. But by 1681, every dodo in the world had died.

_____ 1. From this information, you cannot tell:
    a. whether the people of Concord got the warning
    b. how the people of Concord got the warning
    c. why Paul Revere never made it to Concord
    d. whether Longfellow wrote a good poem

_____ 2. One thing that could be shown in both New York museums is a:
    a. sport fish caught by a lumberman
    b. lock used to secure maple syrup buckets
    c. petrified fish
    d. petrified lumberman

_____ 3. From this information, you can tell that:
    a. parasol ants haven't been named correctly
    b. the ants' jaws stay closed after the ant dies
    c. Native Brazilians named the ants parasol ants
    d. the ants like sunshine

_____ 4. From this story, you can conclude that:
    a. Stacy was sick for three years
    b. Dorsey would never leave Stacy's side
    c. the note told people what to feed Dorsey
    d. Dorsey received a medal from the post office

_____ 5. The story suggests that:
    a. the discovery of the dodo led to its disappearance
    b. the birds were painted for their great beauty
    c. Dutch people are good painters
    d. the dodo came from Europe originally

Unit 22

1. In the seventeenth century the Incas of South America had an empire that stretched over 2,500 miles. They built highways throughout their empire. One of their tunnels went 750 feet through a mountain cliff. A rope suspension bridge of theirs is still used in this century.

2. When it was built in 1940, the Tacoma Narrows Bridge was the world's third largest suspension bridge. Large suspension bridges had been built before. But builders didn't count on the winds near Tacoma, Washington. Four months after its opening, the bridge had blown down.

3. From news reports about Russia, you might think that the Kremlin is a large building in Moscow. Actually, there are many kremlins in Russia. The word means *fortress* in Russian. The Kremlin in Moscow is not one building, but a lot of buildings inside a walled yard.

4. Working at home sounds like fun. You can work in your pajamas, play the radio as loud as you want, and sleep an extra hour in the morning. But making money at home takes drive and dedication. To be successful, you have to apply basic business practices. You can't allow yourself to play rather than work.

5. The Egyptian pyramids were built from stones weighing about two and a half tons each. The structures are 40 stories high. Enough stones were used in each pyramid to build a wall around France. Yet the Egyptians used no animals, had no cranes, and didn't have the wheel.

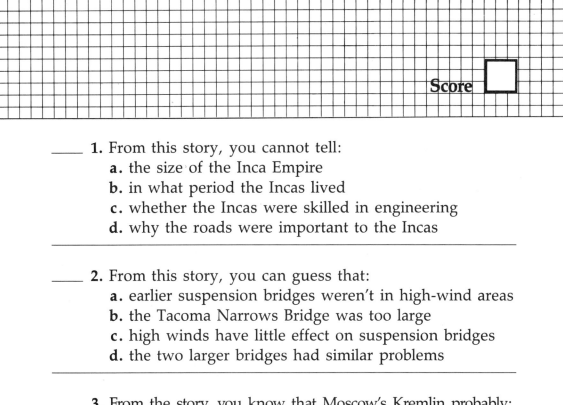

_____ **1.** From this story, you cannot tell:
  a. the size of the Inca Empire
  b. in what period the Incas lived
  c. whether the Incas were skilled in engineering
  d. why the roads were important to the Incas

_____ **2.** From this story, you can guess that:
  a. earlier suspension bridges weren't in high-wind areas
  b. the Tacoma Narrows Bridge was too large
  c. high winds have little effect on suspension bridges
  d. the two larger bridges had similar problems

_____ **3.** From the story, you know that Moscow's Kremlin probably:
  a. is the only one in Russia
  b. is a large building in Russia
  c. was originally a fortress
  d. is never visited by news reporters

_____ **4.** To be successful, you would probably need to:
  a. stock the refrigerator with plenty of food
  b. make a schedule and stick to it
  c. plan when to take naps
  d. work as little as possible

_____ **5.** You can tell from this story that:
  a. the Egyptians built a wall around France
  b. the work must have been done by many people
  c. the pyramids were two and a half stories high
  d. each pyramid weighed about two and a half tons

Unit 23

1.   Water going down a drain forms a funnel that spins in one direction. South of the equator water always turns in a clockwise direction. North of the equator water always turns in the opposite direction. The same effect can be seen in the wind funnels of tornadoes. They spin in opposite directions north and south of the equator.

2.   A caterpillar hangs from a twig using a silk "safety belt" it has spun. Slowly it wiggles out of its old skin without tearing the belt. The caterpillar becomes a pupa. The pupa is very still, but inside changes are happening fast. Finally a black butterfly with orange and white spots rests on the twig that once held its safety belt.

3.   Great Britain may not be the place golf was first played. The ancient Romans played a similar game with a curved stick and a leather ball stuffed with feathers. The Romans occupied Great Britain until 400 A.D.

4.   The Agriculture Department inspects packages from foreign countries. It wants to make sure no plant diseases are brought into the U.S. Dogs have been trained to mix with airline passengers and sniff for food and produce. The dogs sit down by a passenger when they smell food.

5.   One of the worst volcanic eruptions was in 1815. When Mount Tambora blew up, it made a seven-mile hole in the peak. It killed 12,000 people right away. Another 80,000 people later died of hunger. The volcanic ash ruined all the crops.

_____ **1.** From this story you cannot tell:
  a. how water and wind movements are similar
  b. which direction water spins north of the equator
  c. the reason for the differences in direction
  d. which direction a tornado spins south of the equator

_____ **2.** Next, the butterfly probably:
  a. builds a pupa
  b. finds something to eat
  c. swims upstream
  d. becomes a caterpillar

_____ **3.** From this story, you might assume that golf:
  a. began in 400 A.D.
  b. began in Great Britain and moved to Rome
  c. began in Rome and moved to Great Britain
  d. is played more in Rome than Great Britain

_____ **4.** From this information, you can't tell:
  a. why the Agriculture Department inspects packages
  b. how dogs help prevent diseases being brought in
  c. what the dogs do to alert officials to food packages
  d. which foods are not allowed into the country

_____ **5.** From this, you can tell that the greatest danger came:
  a. from the first explosion of the volcano
  b. just before the explosion
  c. after the explosion
  d. within seven miles of the volcano

Score

1. Albert Einstein was once asked in a radio interview whether he got his great thoughts in the bathtub, while walking, or while sitting in his office. Einstein replied, "I don't really know. I've only had one or maybe two."

2. Some people believe there is one place on an airplane that is safer than any other. In case of an accident, however, one place is not much safer than another. Seats in the rear near an exit have some advantage in a head-on crash. But most airplane deaths result from fire and smoke.

3. The special material in our bodies that makes us who we are is called *DNA*. Everybody except identical twins has different DNA. Since DNA is everywhere in the body, scientists believe DNA patterns are better than fingerprints for identifying people.

4. Wind does not push sailboats forward. Instead, the sailboats *fall*. The sails on the boat form a curve when the wind passes across them. The curve creates an empty space behind the sail. The boat goes forward by falling into the empty space.

5. A comet is like a dirty ball of snow. It is made of frozen gases, frozen water, and dust. As a comet approaches the sun, the icy center gets hot and evaporates. The gases made by the evaporation form the tail of the comet. The dust left behind in the process forms meteor showers.

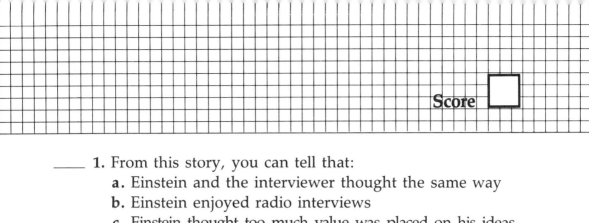

_____ 1. From this story, you can tell that:
   a. Einstein and the interviewer thought the same way
   b. Einstein enjoyed radio interviews
   c. Einstein thought too much value was placed on his ideas
   d. Einstein thought best while walking

_____ 2. From this story, you can tell that:
   a. most airplane deaths are caused by crashes
   b. there's little protection from fire and smoke in a crash
   c. there is one seat in an airplane that is always safe
   d. the safest seat is in front of the wings

_____ 3. From this you can tell that:
   a. some people have the same fingerprints
   b. only identical twins have the same fingerprints
   c. fingerprints are the best way to fight crime
   d. DNA patterns for identical twins are similar

_____ 4. From this story, you cannot tell:
   a. why the sails on a sailboat form a curve
   b. how the sailboat moves forward
   c. how an empty space is created
   d. how the sails are attached to the boat

_____ 5. From this story, you can definitely tell that:
   a. comets are made of snow
   b. if you throw a ball of snow it might become a comet
   c. the sun helps create the tail of the comet
   d. meteor showers are visible from Earth with a
      telescope

53

Unit 25

1. Frank studied his son. He wondered what he could say to convince the boy not to take the job. Frank knew the job seemed wonderful to a boy in high school. How could he explain to his son that it was more important to wait one more year?

2. Clare ran her finger down the first column on the page. "No, no, no," she repeated over and over. Suddenly her finger stopped on one of the little boxes. "Two rooms with a large kitchen," she read. Then she circled the box of print with her pen.

3. Diego sat with his hands clenching the armrests. The woman in the aisle said, "Please fasten your seatbelts." Diego fumbled with the belt. The woman then made sure all the seats were in an upright position. She finished just as the engines began to roar on either side of Diego.

4. The woman happily bounced her grandson on her lap. The baby looked puzzled at first, and then he began to smile. "You had that same little smile when you were his age," the woman said to the man. "I thought I never smiled at that age," the boy's father replied.

5. Louis scraped the black wires with the long fork. He patted three rounded disks of meat until they were smooth. Then he dropped them on the wire. A loud sizzling sound followed. A small cloud of smoke rose from the coals into the branches of the trees overhead.

___ 1. From this, you can tell that the son probably:
   a. needs a job very badly
   b. has one more year to go to finish high school
   c. has been looking for a job for a long time
   d. doesn't make good grades in high school

___ 2. You know from the story that Clare is:
   a. looking in the newspaper for an apartment
   b. studying the outside of an old building
   c. reading a story in the newspaper
   d. writing a story for the newspaper

___ 3. From this, you can tell that Diego probably:
   a. is the son of the woman in the aisle
   b. is on a large bus
   c. is taking his first trip on an airplane
   d. travels often by plane

___ 4. From this, it is clear that the woman:
   a. is the man's sister
   b. is the man's mother
   c. is the man's aunt
   d. is the man's grandmother

___ 5. From this, you can tell that Louis is:
   a. a professional cook in a large restaurant
   b. washing dishes in his home
   c. cooking hamburgers on an outdoor barbecue
   d. cooking hamburgers on a kitchen stove

Conclusion: just for fun

On the Trail of the Bee

The word *bee* appears on each of the lists below. For each list, figure out what a bee has in common with the other things on the list. Then write why you think bee belongs on that list.

List 1

bee

helicopter

plane

bird

_____

_____

_____

_____

List 2

bee

snake

squirrel

robin

_____

_____

_____

_____

List 3

bee

wasp

hornet

mosquito

_____

_____

_____

_____

List 4

bee

flower

grass

tree

_____

_____

_____

_____

What's the Point?

Read each joke. In the space that follows answer the question about why the joke is funny.

1. The school principal received a telephone call. The voice said, "Bob Johnson won't be in school today."
   "Who is this?" asked the principal.
   "This is my father speaking."

   What is the mistake in the phone call?

   _____

   _____

   _____

2. My father was talking to our neighbor. "I'm worried about my daughter's health."
   "Why? What's she got?" asked the neighbor.
   "A motorcycle," answered my father.

   What does the father think of motorcycles?

   _____

   _____

   _____

3. "This is a good restaurant. If you order a fresh egg, you get the freshest egg in the world. If you order hot tea, you get the hottest tea in the world. And . . ."
   "I believe you. I ordered a small steak."

   What is the second person really saying about the steak?

   _____

   _____

   _____

How Are They Alike?

An analogy is a comparison. It points out a relationship between two sets of things. For example:

A *toe* is to a *foot* as a *finger* is to a *hand*.

In other words, a toe is part of a foot just as a finger is part of a hand.

Read each item below. Ask yourself if there is a relationship between the two sets of things. Write *agree* or *disagree* in the box to tell whether you think the analogy makes sense. Then write a reason to explain your conclusion.

1. *Window* is to *house* as *porthole* is to *ship*.

2. *Lace* is to *shoe* as *button* is to *table*.

3. *Trunk* is to *elephant* as *snout* is to *pig*.

4. *Cereal* is to *food* as *baseball* is to *sports*.

5. *Feather* is to *bird* as *fur* is to *car*.

6. *Bush* is to *shrub* as *road* is to *street*.

The Day Begins

Write what you think each day will be like, and state why you think so.

DAY 1

sunshine _____

newspaper on _____
    front steps
_____
color comics
_____
Super Bowl
_____
recipe for chocolate
    cake _____

phone call from _____
    friend
_____

_____

DAY 2

chilly weather _____

ringing alarm clock _____

frozen orange juice _____

last-minute _____
    studying
_____
honking car horn
_____
warm jacket
_____
bag lunch
_____
book bag

exercise clothes

Check yourself

Unit 1	Unit 2	Unit 3	Unit 4	Unit 5	Unit 6	Unit 7	Unit 8
1. c	1. d	1. d	1. c	1. c	1. c	1. b	1. d
2. d	2. d	2. c	2. a	2. b	2. c	2. a	2. c
3. b	3. a	3. b	3. a	3. a	3. a	3. b	3. b
4. a	4. d	4. a	4. d	4. b	4. c	4. c	4. d
5. c	5. a	5. d	5. d	5. d	5. d	5. c	5. b

Unit *9*	Unit *10*	Unit *11*	Unit *12*	Unit *13*	Unit *14*	Unit *15*	Unit *16*
1. c	1. c	1. a	1. d	1. c	1. d	1. c	1. c
2. b	2. c	2. a	2. c	2. c	2. c	2. a	2. a
3. d	3. b	3. c	3. a	3. b	3. c	3. b	3. b
4. c	4. c	4. d	4. b	4. b	4. a	4. d	4. d
5. a	5. d	5. a	5. b	5. a	5. b	5. c	5. d

Unit 17	Unit 18	Unit 19	Unit 20	Unit 21	Unit 22	Unit 23	Unit 24	Unit 25
1. d	1. b	1. d	1. a	1. c	1. d	1. c	1. c	1. b
2. b	2. b	2. b	2. b	2. c	2. a	2. b	2. b	2. a
3. c	3. d	3. d	3. c	3. b	3. c	3. c	3. d	3. c
4. c	4. a	4. d	4. b	4. a	4. b	4. d	4. d	4. b
5. b	5. a	5. d	5. d	5. a	5. b	5. c	5. c	5. c